> Looking Ahead

Introduction by
Terence Riley

The Museum of Modern Art, New York
Distributed by D.A.P. / Distributed Art Publishers, Inc., New York

Produced by the Department of Publications
The Museum of Modern Art, New York
Design and composition by Gina Rossi
Production by Christopher Zichello
Printed and bound by Euro Grafica SpA
Type set in Foundry Monoline and ITC Office
Printed on Biberest Allegro 170 gsm

Library of Congress Control Number: 2002104999
ISBN: 0-87070-685-3

Published by The Museum of Modern Art
11 West 53 Street
New York, New York 10019
www.moma.org
Distributed in the United States and Canada by
D.A.P./Distributed Art Publishers, Inc., New York
Distributed outside the United States and Canada by
Thames & Hudson, Ltd., London

Printed in Italy

Photograph Credits

© Nelson Atkins Museum: 27 top.
© Robert Benson Photography: 29.
Tom Bonner: 22, 23 top left.
Eric van den Brulle: 8-9 (digitally altered), 18, 19 top right.
Cooper, Robertson & Partners: 27 bottom right, 28, 30.
© Esto Photographics, Jeff Goldberg: 31 top right, 31 bottom
right.
© Esto Photographics, Peter Mauss: 31 left.
Elizabeth Felicella: 2-3 (digitally altered), 6, 14, 15 top, 16-17
(digitally altered), 19 top left, 19 bottom.
Michael Maltzan Architecture, Inc.: 10, 11, 12, 13, 15 bottom
(digitally altered), 21, 23 bottom right, 25.
© E. G, Schempf: 27 bottom left.
Joshua White: 24.

**FRANCIS CLOSE HALL
LEARNING CENTRE**
Swindon Road, Cheltenham
Gloucestershire GL50 4AZ
Telephone: 01242 714600

UNIVERSITY OF
GLOUCESTERSHIRE
at Cheltenham and Gloucester

NORMAL LOAN

420 3/2011

> Contents

On behalf of the Trustees and staff of The Museum of Modern Art, I am pleased to welcome New Yorkers and other visitors to the Museum's splendid new multi-use facility in Long Island City, Queens, where MoMA's exciting program of modern and contemporary art continues to move forward during the major expansion and rebuilding of the Museum in Manhattan. There, a magnificent new structure designed by Yoshio Taniguchi will rise on a site adjoining the Museum. Scheduled for completion in 2005, the new Museum of Modern Art, along with the renovated 1939 building and 1953 sculpture garden, will have greatly enlarged gallery spaces, educational facilities, offices, and public areas.

The realization of MoMA QNS, the new facility in Long Island City, a short subway, bus, or automobile ride from our Museum in Manhattan, enables MoMA to remain a vital force within the city's art community and continue to serve the public with special exhibitions and with familiar masterworks from its unrivaled collection. MoMA QNS joins its partner, P.S. 1, and other cultural institutions in Long Island City. Our new building has been superbly designed by Cooper Robertson & Partners and Michael Maltzan Architecture, Inc. It combines state-of-the-art climate-controlled art storage, and conservation and photographic imaging facilities, which will remain in use after the opening of the Taniguchi building, with handsome new galleries, bookstore, café, and other visitor services.

The following pages feature the MoMA QNS building and the architects who made it. We are deeply grateful to them and their associates for their extraordinary efforts in creating a fine facility worthy of this Museum. We are especially indebted to the extraordinary Museum staff members for their fine work and heroic efforts in a difficult time of transition. Finally, but in no way last in importance, we owe the success of this historic moment in the Museum's history to its Board of Trustees, led by Ronald S. Lauder and Agnes Gund, and to its other supporters whose generosity and guiding counsel have made the entire enterprise possible.

Glenn D. Lowry, Director
The Museum of Modern Art, New York

The Museum of Modern Art's new facility in Long Island City, formerly a 170,000-square-foot stapler factory, has been designed both as a temporary exhibition presence and a long-term art storage facility in the borough of Queens. The public areas, which include 25,000 square feet of gallery space and visitor amenities, and support spaces, such as a conservation lab, carpentry shops, and registrar areas, will serve as the temporary home of the Museum's exhibition program for three years, while the Museum's Manhattan facility is greatly expanded and renovated. MoMA QNS also accommodates a wide range of functions that will continue to operate and grow over the years after the Museum's main exhibition program moves back to West Fifty-third Street.

The permanent functions include study centers, library facilities, digital imaging resources, and climate-controlled storage, according to the architectural plan designed by the New York City firm Cooper, Robertson & Partners. The study centers will accommodate the growing number of scholars who request access to the Museum's extensive collections, library, archives, and other scholarly resources. The majority of these programs will continue to operate at MoMA QNS, with ample room to grow over the years, after the Museum reopens its rebuilt facility in Manhattan.

The exterior of the MoMA QNS building and its interior public spaces were designed by the Los Angeles firm Michael Maltzan Architecture, Inc. The facades of the building have been resurfaced to ensure the interior climate control crucial for art storage, and delineated horizontally to emphasize the low-rise character of Long Island City, an environment that Maltzan has described as a "middle landscape," where the high density of the city meets the sprawl of suburbia. A band of white stucco hugs the street level above which a bright blue band, recalling the blue glazed brick of the former stapler factory, encircles the building. On the principal facade along Thirty-third Street a beam of light extends above the sidewalk, leading visitors from the nearby subway station and bus stop to the mid-block, etched-glass entrance to the public spaces.

In recognition of the fact that the elevated subway line adjacent to MoMA QNS is the strongest physical landmark in the area and a symbol of the temporary Museum's accessibility and its links to audiences both in Manhattan and the so-called outer boroughs, Maltzan treated the roof surface, clearly visible from the trains, as a principal feature of his design. The roofscape comprises the usual required mechanical equipment and stairway bulkheads, which are rendered in a matte black, and the contrasting reflective surfaces of the Museum's typographical logo, MoMA QNS, seemingly fragmented and scattered on them in a random fashion. But from the vantage point of an approaching train, the fractured logo type momentarily comes together and announces MoMA's presence just before the train enters the station.

> MoMA QNS rooftop as seen from the 7 local train

The themes of time, motion, and the experiential event are carried throughout the design of MoMA's temporary museum. Indeed, the three-letter suffix of the facility's name—QNS—is the Metropolitan Transit Authority designation for the borough of Queens. The seamless rising and falling of the subway lines above and below the city are further reflected in Maltzan's design for the entry to the public spaces of the Museum. Upon arriving at the mid-block entrance, the visitor climbs a short flight of stairs above a former loading dock, then descends a gently sloping ramp to the main ticketing area. Soaring above this area is a space dedicated to installations of contemporary art. A mezzanine, reached by a winding ramp on one end and a shallow stair on the other, wraps continuously around the main space in a contrapuntal fashion, energizing it as a seemingly endless passage. Here the visitor finds a coatroom, café, bookstore, and other services.

The entry sequence flows imperceptibly into lofty galleries, which reflect both the cool abstraction of MoMA's traditional exhibition spaces as well as the industrial character of the former manufacturing space. Darkened ceilings with exposed mechanical works and lighting grids hover above the 20-foot-high exhibition spaces and polished concrete floors. The structure's original twenty-five-foot column bay accommodates a flexible disposition of freestanding partitions for various types of exhibitions.

The former stapler factory's large floor plates and ample column bay were also utilized by Scott Newman, of Cooper, Robertson & Partners, in his superb design for the building's permanent study centers, library, archives, art storage and conservation facilities, digital-imaging, and other semi-public and staff spaces. Wide corridors allow the free movement of art between conservation, storage, and shipping areas, which are all connected vertically by a 12 x 19-foot freight elevator. Newman also took advantage of the structure's generous height in inserting a second floor, or mezzanine, above a portion of the upper level, creating a focal point for the study-center functions. His unique design provides a reading room and other facilities for resident and visiting scholars who wish to explore the Museum's vast resources for research in modern and contemporary art.

The MoMA QNS building, shown on the following pages, succeeds architecturally on a number of levels: as a sensitive and handsome design by expert architects, as an ingenious solution to the practical challenges of a growing institution, and as a symbolic expression of the Museum's original mandate, to enable the public to "enjoy, understand and use the visual arts of our time."

Terence Riley, Chief Curator,
Department of Architecture and Design

> east elevation

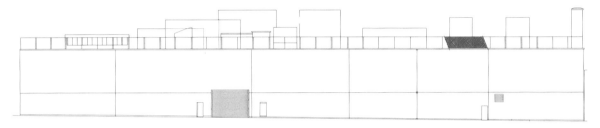

> west elevation

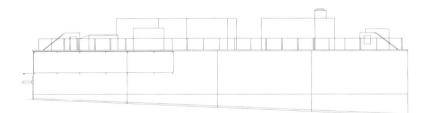

> north elevation

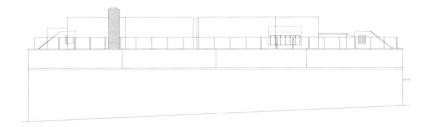

> south elevation

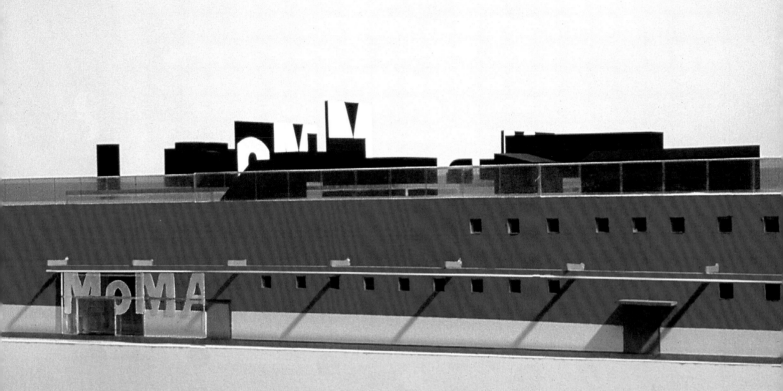

model showing entrance facade

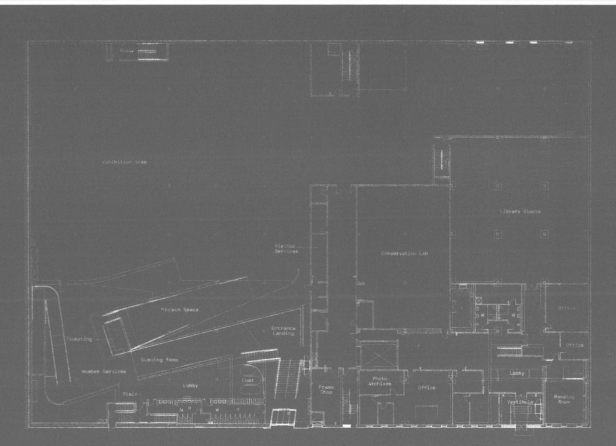

> first-floor plan

> model, overhead view of interior

> computer view, ticketing desk with exhibition space above it

> model, entrance

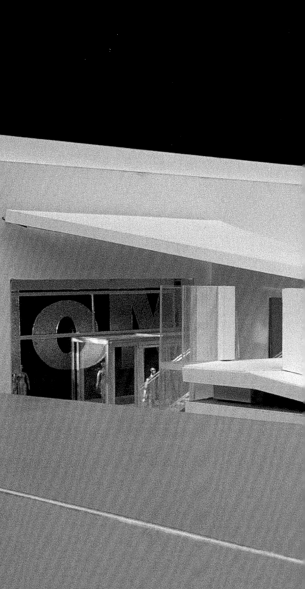

> model, lobby view from galleries

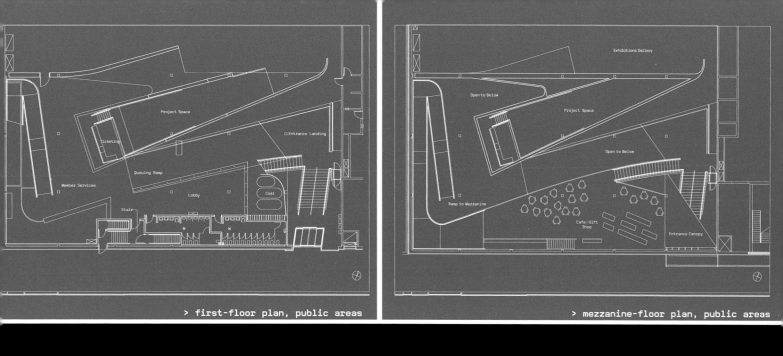

> first-floor plan, public areas

> mezzanine-floor plan, public areas

> entrance ramp in construction, view from mezzanine

> entrance stair in construction

> corridor in construction

> scaffolding on entrance facade

> roofscape

> entrance

> entrance ramp

> entrance ramp from mezzanine

> ticketing desk from mezzanine

iew toward galleries

> ticketing desk

Michael Maltzan Architecture, Inc.

Michael Maltzan Architecture, Inc., established in 1995 by Michael T. Maltzan, is a Los Angeles architecture firm known for its innovative design work on a wide range of arts, educational, commercial, institutional, and residential projects. The firm is the recipient of a number of honor awards, including design awards from the American Institute of Architects for the Feldman/Horn Center for the Arts, Los Angeles, and the Hergott Shepard Residence, Beverly Hills, and a *Progressive Architecture* award for the Inner-City Arts Campus expansion in Los Angeles. Maltzan received the Young Architects Award from the Architectural League in 1999.

In addition to the firm's design work for MoMA QNS, the temporary home of The Museum of Modern Art in Queens, it has served as the architect for the Mark Taper Center/Inner-City Arts Campus, the Harvard/Westlake School's Feldman/Horn Center for the Arts, and the Getty Information Institute's Digital Laboratory, all in Los Angeles; the UCLA Hammer Museum Art and Cultural Center in Los Angeles (with Bruce Mau of Toronto and Petra Blaisse of the Netherlands); and the Kidspace Museum for children in Pasadena, California.

The work of Michael Maltzan Architecture, Inc., has been featured in numerous publications and exhibited widely, at the Municipal Art Society in New York, the Graduate School of Design, Harvard University, in Cambridge, Massachusetts, and the Museum of Contemporary Art in Los Angeles. The Hergott Shepard Residence was included in *The Un-Private House* exhibition at The Museum of Modern Art, which was subsequently seen in Vienna, Minneapolis, Los Angeles, and Barcelona.

Maltzan studied at the Rhode Island School of Design, Providence, and the Graduate School of Design at Harvard University, and has taught and served as visiting critic at The Architectural League of New York, Rhode Island School of Design, University of California at Los Angeles, University of Southern California, Harvard University, University of Waterloo, and the Southern California Institute of Architecture.

The UCLA Hammer Museum Art and Cultural Center
Los Angeles, California. 2003

The UCLA Hammer Museum Art and Cultural Center offers collections, exhibitions, and cultural programs, with a special emphasis on contemporary art. It is housed in a 1990 building characterized by blank and seemingly impervious facades, and several entrances. The museum is situated at an urban crossroads within the city, but suffers from anonymity. It is located along Wilshire Boulevard, south of the UCLA campus and Westwood Village. Positioned between two distinct morphologies, the campus and the continuous grid of Los Angeles to the south, the museum is potentially a critical threshold within the city's cultural life.

Thus, the strategy for the project was to develop a more integrated identity for the museum, both externally and internally. The architects believed a broad architectural scope was needed for so complex and promising a project, and created a collaborative team of intellectual partners to unite traditionally distinct disciplines in a focused strategy for significant intervention to solve the museum's multivalent issues, including Bruce Mau (graphics), Petra Blaisse (landscape), and Paul Zaferiou (lighting).

At the center of the design, a new bridge and stair physically and metaphorically link the courtyard to the galleries. Tying exhibitions, as well as the two main facades, together, the bridge allows the museum to develop more integrated programming. The two sides of the museum are linked at the public interior courtyard, which is accessible via two unique paths (one from parking and Wilshire Boulevard, the other from Westwood Village). This space is further enhanced by the addition of a 300-seat theater, restaurant, bookstore, and public classroom.

An iconographic and disparate strategy of luminous and translucent elements creates orientation markers, provides signage opportunities for describing museum content, and creates a sense of transparency against the closed quality of the existing building. This is clearest in the continuous iconographic light pattern, which begins on the parking level, appears at key moments, and finally becomes a canopy for the upper level of the bridge.

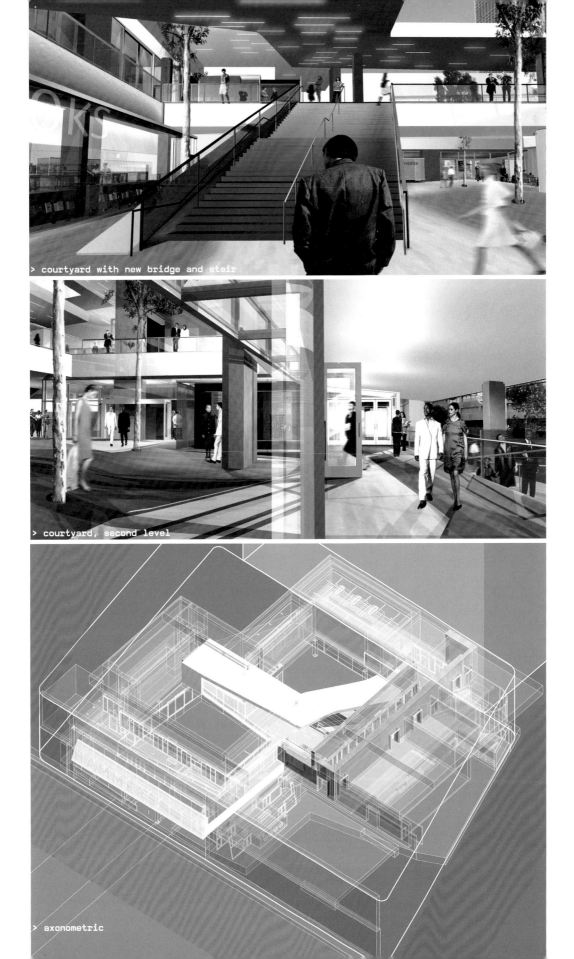

> courtyard with new bridge and stair

> courtyard, second level

> axonometric

The new Feldman/Horn Center for the Arts was created by Michael Maltzan Architecture, Inc., to bring together different components of Harvard/Westlake's Department of Art, which for years had been spread over its campus in makeshift spaces. The school's most significant building, a historic chapel, is located at one end of the project site, where a new art gallery provides an important venue on campus for student and professional artists.

In order to reintegrate the overall campus infrastructure, the architects considered both the existing structures and the planned expansion to the west of the site, and concluded that the 23,800 square-foot Center for the Arts should act as a transitional public space, rather than just a destination. Given the inherent complexities of the spatial and built conditions on and adjacent to the project, a traditional campus plan would have been inappropriate. Instead, a new spatial structure and organization was proposed that was defined by movement through space rather than occupation of it.

This armature of movement uses a new tower as an orienting device to establish visual connections throughout the Center from each of its several entry points. These thresholds at first present an image of formal complexity, which gives way to a more continuous, open, and expansive common public space within the courtyard.

Relationships with the surrounding buildings are fostered through a series of geometric and dimensional, as well as metaphoric, connections. The existing use of stucco throughout the campus is reiterated in the new buildings in terms of its common volumetric and massive qualities, and it is explored further in terms of its potential thinness expressing a building's "skin."

> tower, from the northwest

> tower, from the southwest

courtyard, from the west

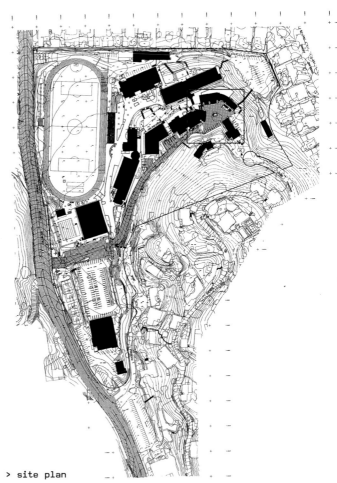

> site plan

The new Kidspace Museum will be located in Brookside Park on three acres of gently sloping, forested land. This landmark site includes three historic Fannie Morrison Horticultural Center buildings constructed in 1938. A fourth, lost to fire in 1984, will be replaced by new buildings that redefine the existing courtyard while providing views into the park between and through the new structure.

The entry to the museum, formerly a passageway through one of the buildings, has been reconfigured to draw visitors up to a raised plinth that overlooks the courtyard. Each building opens onto the courtyard to encourage visitors to move back and forth between enclosed, programmed spaces and open vistas.

Permanent exhibits are housed in an existing octagonal building, as well as in the new structure. New gallery space exists on several levels, all of which are visually and physically connected. A tilted tower element in the northwest corner shelters a climbing structure for children from which they can view various perspectives of the surrounding context. Beneath the new temporary-exhibition galleries, the sloping courtyard leads to a 100-seat, multi-form theater. When weather permits, large sliding glass doors transform the space into a semi-outdoor amphitheater. Administrative offices are located in an existing building directly across the courtyard from the new museum, while the front building houses an early-childhood development classroom, a café, and a gift shop.

Sensitivity to building heights, alignments, and views creates interesting relationships between the existing and the new, and materials used in the existing buildings are repeated in the new structures at differing scales and textures. However, the design of the new 45,000 square-foot museum by Michael Maltzan Architects, Inc., does not mimic or replicate the style of these older buildings. The architecture confidently represents the present, with respect for the past and an optimistic nod toward the future.

> model, view from above

> model, interior

Cooper, Robertson & Partners

Cooper, Robertson & Partners is a full-service architecture firm with an extensive portfolio of work for cultural institutions. Founded in 1979 by Alexander Cooper, the New York firm has a diverse portfolio of work, equally divided among architectural projects, urban design, and master planning. The firm has been the recipient of numerous design awards, including the National Institute of Architects Honor Award in both architecture and urban design, as well as several awards from the Urban Land Institute, which gave its Award for Excellence for the firm's work on Celebration, a new town in Florida.

Recognized for its expertise in museum planning and design, Cooper, Robertson & Partners has worked with The Museum of Modern Art for six years on a number of projects, culminating in its role as executive architect for the building at MoMA QNS.

In New York, the firm has provided architectural services to such institutions as the Museum of the City of New York, the American Museum of the Moving Image, Lincoln Center (New York State Theater, New York City Ballet, New York City Opera), The City Center for Music and Drama, New York Botanical Garden, Brooklyn Botanical Garden, the Whitney Museum of American Art, and the Solomon R. Guggenheim Foundation.

Cooper, Robertson & Partners is also involved in numerous institutional projects outside New York, including master plans for the Seattle Art Museum and a new visitors center at Monticello for the Thomas Jefferson Memorial Foundation in Charlottesville, Virginia; design of the Shaker Museum in Mt. Lebanon, New York; a new museum and visitors center at the Gettysburg National Military Park in Pennsylvania; and the Institute for the Arts and Humanities at the University of North Carolina at Chapel Hill.

> Henry Moore Sculpture Garden, Nelson-Atkins Museum of Art
> Kansas City, Missouri. 1988

Cooper, Robertson & Partners, in association with landscape architect Daniel Urban Kiley, won a national competition to prepare a master plan for the 46-acre grounds of the Nelson-Atkins Museum of Art and design a sculpture garden for a large collection of bronzes by Henry Moore. The selection of the site for the sculpture garden was part of the planning process, which also included developing options for a 160,000 square-foot building expansion and assessing current and future parking needs.

The goals for the sculpture garden were an informal yet private setting for the sculptures and an enhanced definition of the south mall, the museum's principal open space. Two allées of linden and crabapple trees were set along the lawn's north-south axis to create the basic garden structure. Stone walking paths run along the allées, and extend beyond the trees, gradually climbing through bosques of gingko trees set in a series of grass and yew terraces to reach the museum's grand southern steps.

Twelve Henry Moore sculptures, comprising one of the finest collections in the world, were sited in two wooded groves flanking the mall. The design of the groves was based on the preexisting nature of the site, and allows each sculpture to be revealed in sequence within the garden, yet retain its individuality. The garden reinforces and enhances the presence of the museum and its grounds as an important element among Kansas City's public spaces, fully integrating them into the city's park system. In 1994 the architects assisted the museum in siting a major addition to the Henry Moore Sculpture Garden, an installation by Claes Oldenburg and Coosje van Bruggen titled *Shuttlecocks*.

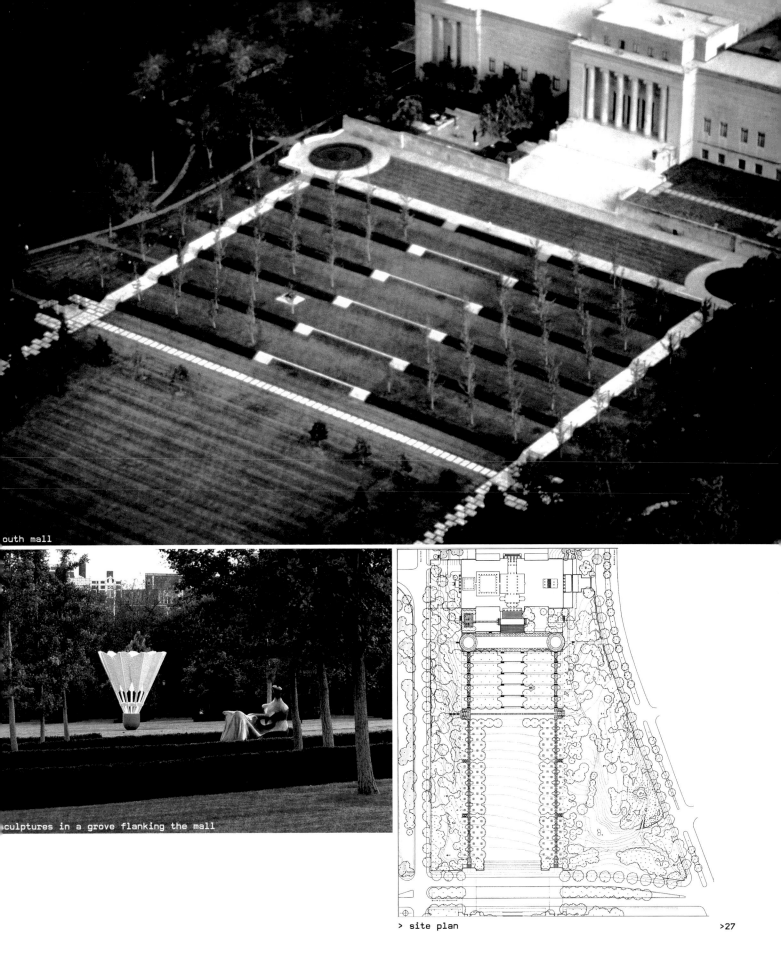

outh mall

culptures in a grove flanking the mall

> site plan

The Ohio State University originally asked Cooper, Robertson & Partners to provide master planning and programming for a new College of Business. A comprehensive study of an 11-acre site on the northern edge of the campus analyzed traffic, parking, pedestrian circulation, open space, and site utilities and regulations. After developing a full Program of Requirements for the college, the architects found that only half the offered site was necessary to meet the business college's needs; the other half could be returned to the university for other uses. The master plan created an ensemble of interconnected buildings, extending the established neoclassical architectural vocabulary of the campus.

Once the master plan was approved by Ohio State, the architects were selected jointly with Kallman McKinnell Wood as design architects for the quadrangle's six buildings. Cooper, Robertson & Partners were to design three of the buildings, Fisher Hall, the Pfahl Executive Education Building, and the Executive Residence. The architectural elements articulated in the master plan served as guiding principles for each building's design. These included two academic quadrangles, the use of a simple rectangular plan, massing of three to four story buildings, symmetrically balanced facade compositions, a rusticated stone base with two-story middle with double height windows and columns, and an articulated cornice or clerestory floor. Roofs are pitched with standing seam copper ribs to provide a strong profile. Wall materials are blended brick with stone trim, both in earth tone colors.

Fisher Hall, completed in 1998, is 127,000 square feet and serves as the academic and administrative center for the new campus. The Pfahl Executive Education Center, which opened in 1999, is 60,000 square feet of classrooms, lecture halls, an auditorium, and flexible rooms for executive training programs. The Executive Residence will be a 179,000 square foot residential building for business executives while they are attending programs at the College of Business.

> model, view from above

ampus view

> campus view

ampus view

Stuyvesant High School is a New York City public school specializing in mathematics and science that provides university-level facilities for 3,000 students. The project serves as a standard for high-school design and construction in New York City; the entire process, from site selection to occupancy, which typically takes eight years, was accomplished by Cooper, Robertson & Partners in four and a half years.

The high-rise school building, a vertical stack of ten floors, was a response to its small triangular site at the northernmost end of a residential community at Battery Park City. The 406,00 square-foot building features a classroom/laboratory wing, consisting of computer and science laboratories, and a workshop/classroom wing positioned on either side of a central section containing a swimming pool, two gymnasia, a multiple-use auditorium, and a cafeteria. These are public spaces, which received a high priority; special attention given to providing community access to the ground-floor activity spaces.

The interior spaces include flexible layouts for classrooms and laboratories, pre-wired into computer and audio-visual intercom networks, with a satellite broadcast link for transmitting and receiving. The Stuyvesant High School building has received numerous design awards and has become an integral part of Lower Manhattan.

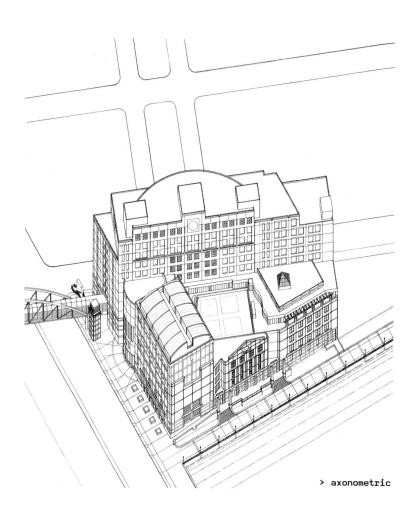

> axonometric

> escalators

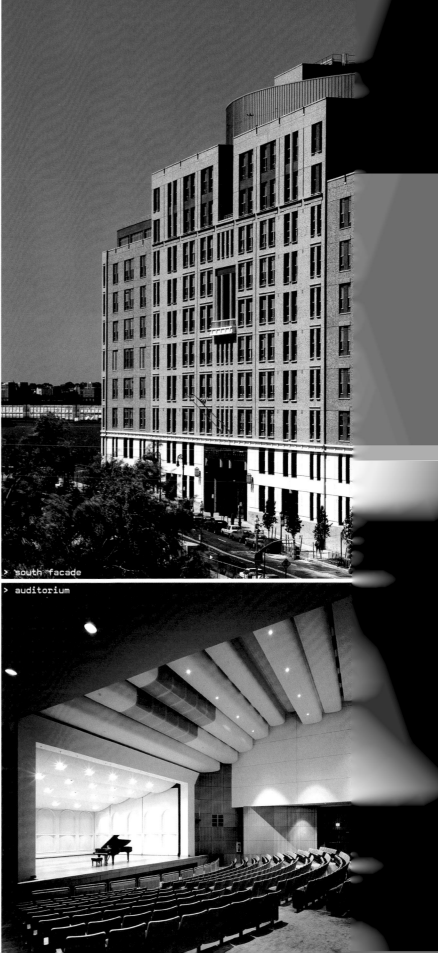

> south facade

> auditorium